Philip Aryee

SECURITY CHALLENGES IN IMPLICATION OF EDGE COMPUTING

Philip Aryee

SECURITY CHALLENGES IN IMPLICATION OF EDGE COMPUTING

IN NIGERIAN EDUCATIONAL INSTITUTIONS

LAP LAMBERT Academic Publishing

Imprint

Cover image: www.ingimage.com

Publisher:
LAP LAMBERT Academic Publishing
is a trademark of
Dodo Books Indian Ocean Ltd. and OmniScriptum S.R.L publishing group

120 High Road, East Finchley, London, N2 9ED, United Kingdom
Str. Armeneasca 28/1, office 1, Chisinau MD-2012, Republic of Moldova, Europe
Managing Directors: Ieva Konstantinova, Victoria Ursu
info@omniscriptum.com

Printed at: see last page
ISBN: 978-620-8-49817-7

SECURITY CHALLENGES IN IMPLICATION OF EDGE COMPUTING IN NIGERIAN EDUCATIONAL INSTITUTIONS

Dr. Swapna H. R
Professor
Department of Commerce-PG Studies
School of Commerce
JAIN (Deemed-to-be University)
swapna.hulimavu@gmail.com

Philip Aryee
School of Commerce- PG Studies
JAIN (Deemed-to-be University)
paryee@rocketmail.com
_+233-240081392_

Atanda Sheu Adeleke
School of Commerce- PG Studies
JAIN (Deemed-to-be University)
atandasheu@gmail.com
_+234-8167269024_

ACKNOWLEGMENT

We thank the Lord Almighty for giving us the wisdom and insights to change the lives of countless millions through the writing of this book.

We thank our parents for helping us shape the life with positivity and passion. Without you, we would never have been the person who we are today. Thank you for everything! The sacrifices you've made are beyond any description. Thank you, my beloveds. I hope to make you proud someday.

TABLE OF CONTENT

LIST OF TABLES

LIST OF GRAPHS

ABSTRACT

Using the Internet to link and monitor real-world items (things) is referred to as the Internet of Things (IoT). In terms of our home, we may leverage this principle to make it more intelligent, secure, and automated. It is the goal of this Internet-of-things project to create a smart wireless home security system that notifies its owner through the Internet if anybody attempts to enter the property without permission, and can also raise an alarm if necessary. It is also possible to use the same set of sensors for home automation. It is possible for the user to get warnings and status updates from the WiFi-connected microcontroller-managed system on his phone from a distance, regardless of whether his phone is connected to the internet, since this system is preferred over current systems of a similar kind. An inbuilt Wi-Fi shield and an embedded microcontroller are utilized in the present prototype to control and manage all of the home's electrical appliances. TI-CC3200 Launchpad board

Key Words: *Edge computing, Computer-assistance, Internet of Things (IoT), Educational institution, Nigeria*

CHAPTER ONE
INTRODUCTION

CHAPTER 1

INTRODUCTION

1.1 THEORETICAL BACKGROUND

Innovative and structural ideals that seek to create various applications that are now part of our everyday routine of life might be described as the IoT (internet of things). More than a hundred million smart devices are linked together in massive networks that enable a wide range of vital functions, such as communication between systems and the tracking and management of key infrastructures. As a result of the rapid expansion of IoT devices, as well as the resulting surge in data traffic produced at the network's edge, there have been new strains placed on the system's incapacity to handle the increased data traffic. In this regard, edge computing (EC) has emerged as a novel approach to bring processing and storage closer to the end users, which we have dubbed edge computing-assisting IoT. Data security and privacy are major concerns with this issue, despite its unique features and improved Quality of Service (QoS). EC-assisted IoT has unique security and privacy difficulties, and this study examines them in depth. As a first step, we provide an overview of EC-aided IoT, which includes definitions of the technology and its applications, architecture, benefits and disadvantages. EC-assisted IoT security and privacy are defined in this context. As a follow-up, we go into great detail on the many types of attacks that may be launched against EC-assisted IoT devices, as well as viable solutions and defences. Based on security services and security goals, we then categorise a number of security and privacy concerns that are explored in the literature in this manner. Many outstanding issues and possible future avenues for the secure EC-assisted IoT paradigm are also fully discussed in this article. An IoT device is a collection of smart devices that include sensors and actuators that communicate, store, and receive data through the internet. New novel services and applications may now be supported by IoT devices due to the fast growth of information technology (IT). Because of advances in data processing, transmission, and pervasiveness of wireless networks, the number of edge devices has skyrocketed in recent years. By 2025, it is predicted that 180ZBytes of data would be generated as a result of the ever-increasing edge devices. The International Data Corporation - IDC – estimates this. International Data Corporation (IDC) estimates that the number of edge devices will approach 150 billion and the data generated by these devices would account for 70 percent of the data produced globally by the end of 2017. In light of the need for IoT devices to work in conjunction with other emerging technologies such as big data, artificial intelligence, mobile computing, and so on, it is clearly evident that centralized processing of any sort will be unable to support this innovative computing paradigm. The edge computing-aided Internet of Things (IoT) might alleviate these issues. A combination of cloud computing and edge computing is used to overcome the issues outlined above in IoT-assisted edge computing. It has been more popular in academic and industrial circles in recent years. It connects cloud computing facilities and services to the end users, enabling numerous upcoming technologies including as 5G, the Internet of Things (IoT), augmented reality, and vehicle-to-vehicle communications. Delay-sensitive applications may benefit from Edge computing's reduced latency, mobility, and position awareness. The newest breakthroughs in edge computing, such as Mobile Edge Computing, Cloudlet, and Fog computing, have been evaluated in order to provide academics with a better understanding of the current solutions and potential applications. As a complete assessment of current Edge computing breakthroughs, this article focuses on the fundamental applications. An important aspect of real-world application reaction time is discussed in this article as well. Ending with a discussion of open Edge computing research problems and needs, the paper comes to a conclusion.

1.2 INDUSTRY OVERVIEW

Why Edge Computing-Assisted Internet of Things

There is a tremendous quantity of data being created in a wide range of industries as the world moves toward digitalization. However, in most cases, this data must be processed fast in order to keep up with current technological developments (real-time applications). Small and medium-sized enterprises and research institutions no longer need to own their own computers to do computations thanks to cloud technology, which was introduced some years ago. There is still a need for users to transmit and receive data between the machine's physical location and the end user's location. Another method for doing computations close to the data is edge computing, which may be used for real-time applications. In contrast to cloud computing and supercomputers, edge computing is not a direct competition, although it does share computational loads with these technologies.

The reasons for implementing edge computing are outlined in the following sections:

- Push from the cloud services: In general, cloud computing has shown to be quite effective in terms calculations, but in certain instances, there needs to be an alternate method to prevent data transmission bottlenecks. This issue is being addressed via edge computing. Boeing's 787 creates 5GBs of data per minute, and sending this data to the ground via a satellite is inefficient for data processing, as shown by the example.
- Push from the internet of things: Is a major factor in this, the Internet of Things (IoT) now includes electrical devices such as LEDs, security cameras, and air quality sensors, which generate and consume a lot of data. More and more electrical gadgets will be linked to the Internet of Things (IoT) in the future. Data processing on the cloud is not possible because of bandwidth and latency issues. Edge devices will have to process part of the information.

- Communication: EC-assisted IoT networks have improved network performance in terms of decreased latency (both communication and computation), reduced bandwidth utilisation, lower device power consumption, and reduced packet data overhead.
- (W. Yu et al., 2018) (B. Omoniwa,2018). For IoT applications and services that demand a high quality of service (QoS) at all times, the overall network performance is greatly improved.
- (J. Pan et al., 2018) Processing: Edge servers in EC-assisted IoT networks will take over data processing and computation from cloud servers, freeing them up for other tasks. Improved resource utilization and priority management are ensured as a result. Storage:
- EC servers offer storage services to IoT end devices because to the restricted storage capabilities of these devices.
- Transferring all data generated or acquired by the devices to storage servers is the method used to achieve this end result. This will help with the management of load balancing and failure recovery issues, resulting in a significant increase in Quality of Service.

1.3 BACKGROUND OF THE STUDY

Definition of Security and Privacy in the Context of EC-Assisted IoT

(D. He, S. Chan, 2018) Edge IoT solutions are able to handle enormous amounts of data at the network's perimeter. Low- or high-sensitive apps and services from different vertical IoT areas may include this information. IoT systems that employ electric current are often implemented via public or private networks to transfer data between end devices and cloud system EC nodes.

Because none of these EC-aided software systems are secure from significant security and privacy problems and attacks, they are all vulnerable. The increasing complexity of IoT networks also increases the security difficulties encountered by such networks.

X. Xiaohui, (2013) As a result of the vast quantity of devices and data created by IoT networks, these networks are very difficult to maintain. Attacks on IoT networks are conceivable due to the devices' accessibility.

Once the hacked node is in the hands of the hackers, they may use it to carry out their nefarious operations and target other devices nearby. Internet of Things (IoT) devices do not contain anti-virus or anti-malware software. This is a result of the devices' low memory and power consumption. The lack of virus and malware security on IoT devices makes them very vulnerable to becoming bots and causing harm to other devices in the network. Once an IoT device has been compromised, the hacker has access to the device's routing and forwarding functions. Attackers may acquire access to sensitive data broadcast and gathered by IoT devices as well as other devices in the network.

A. Kanuparthi, (2013) The broad use of IoT might be hampered if data is not protected with confidentiality, integrity, and security. Due to the limited resources of IoT networks, methods for attack mitigation and privacy protection developed for conventional networks cannot be easily applied to IoT networks. This has been made abundantly clear in the conversation that has taken place so far.

Challenges of Edge-Assisted IoT

The use of EC-assisted IoT architecture has significant advantages, but it also has several drawbacks.

• Security and privacy: IoT architecture with EC assistance has multiple advantages, but also many drawbacks. the European Commission will confront new and unanticipated security and privacy threats. IoT functionality demands the transfer of services between the local and global scales, which exposes the network to malicious activities. Furthermore, since sensitive private information will be shared and/or stored on EC servers, security and privacy become key issues in a distributed system. This makes EC-aided IoT networks more vulnerable to cyberattacks and threats. Communication, computation, and storage—three of EC servers' most important functions—all have the potential to be targets for malicious attacks.

• heterogeneity of the network: IoT networks powered by EC are heterogeneous in that they incorporate various network topologies, hardware platforms, and servers.

As a consequence, ensuring that IoT devices work smoothly in such a complex and sophisticated environment is one of the primary challenges. The ability to manage and program resources across a wide range of physical systems, for example, would be problematic.

• Resource management: The ability to manage and program resources across a wide range of physical systems, for example, would be very challenging. An important challenge in controlling the three key resources (communication, computation and storage) in the decentralized EC-assisted IoT is resource management. This must be carefully explored and addressed. As a consequence of the wide range of service providers, IoT edge devices, and applications, this issue has emerged.

• Smart system support: With the convergence of smart IoT devices like sensors and actuators, new options for data collecting, resource allocation and optimization, and system management will emerge. In spite of this, the challenge remains to ensure that a big number of EC servers/nodes can store, analyze, and share the collected data flow from these multi-platform devices dispersed over wide geographic areas in a manner that guarantees optimal and timely management decisions.

Classifications Based On Security and Privacy Attacks and Threats

• EC-aided IoT networks (EC devices, communication and EC servers/nodes and cloud servers) face many security and privacy concerns, and this section focuses on the most likely types and sources of these vulnerabilities.

• Malicious hardware/Software infection: It is possible for attackers to infiltrate the EC servers using malicious software or hardware components installed at the communication and EC nodes levels. There are a number of ways that adversaries might exploit service providers, such as stealing data or reporting false data. They can even betray the integrity of databases. Hardware injection attacks can in a wide variety of forms, including:

a. new malicious EC node is inserted into the network, and an ID number is assigned to it that is a copy of an already approved node. Data packets that are intercepted by the malicious copy may be corrupted, stolen, or misdirected by an attacker as a consequence. It is also possible for node replicas to deactivate and remove valid ECNodes by using node-revocation protocols.

b. To get access to data or software running on these ICs, hackers might use a hardware Trojan, which is an illicit entry into integrated circuits (ICs). In general, there are two sorts of Trojans: those that are triggered from inside the system, and those that are activated by sensors or antennas attached to the system.
c. Attackers may use camouflage, in which they create and use a false node in the network that seems to be an authentic EC node in terms of creating and exchanging data packets.
• False data packets may be injected into the network, or legitimate data packets may be prevented from being sent entirely, by EC nodes that are corrupted or malicious.
• Jamming attacks: Forged communications overwhelm the network in order to decrease communication, processing, or storage capacity. As a consequence, authorized users of the EC-assisted IoT network will be unable to access its infrastructure.
• DDoS attacks, also known as distributed denial of service attacks: Outage attacks, sleep deprivation, and battery depletion are among the most common DDoS assaults against EC nodes. EC nodes are unable to perform their normal activities during outage attacks because they have been exposed to unauthorized access. Sleep deprivation leads to EC nodes being inundated with a large number of legitimate requests. Detecting such an attack is far more challenging. Battery depletion results in the failure or outage of EC nodes and sensors/devices. While signal jamming is the most common DDoS attack at the communication level, EC nodes sending or receiving packets on a regular basis also engage in continuous jamming across all channels.

• Physical Attacks or Tampering: When an attacker has physical access to an EC node or device, they may perform an attack called "physical attacks" or "tampering." An attack on the cryptographic data might compromise the system's integrity and allow for changes to the software or operating system.

Eavesdropping or Sniffing: Secretly listening in on private conversations such as usernames and passwords through communication channels is one of the most common methods of eavesdropping or sniffing by opponents. Assailants may get access to the shared network password and node configuration by intercepting messages containing EC node access or control information.

• Non-network side-channel attack: may disclose critical information even if the EC nodes aren't sending or receiving any data. This might lead to serious privacy problems, for example, if recognized electromagnetic/acoustic signals or protocols from medical equipment are detected.

• Routing Information Attacks: Data packets may be diverted or deleted by attackers to alter routing information at the communication level. When a high-powered, malicious EC-node broadcasts 'HELLO PACKETS' to all nodes claiming to be its neighbors and drains all network packets, it is a Black Hole. When a Gray Hole drains only some network packets, it is a Worm Hole. When an attacker records network packets at one location and then migrates them, it is the Gray Hole.
When a high-powered, malicious EC-node broadcasts 'HELLO PACKETS' to all nodes claiming to be its neighbours and drains all network packets, it is a Black Hole. When a Gray Hole drains only some network packets, it is a Worm Hole. When an attacker records network packets at one location and then migrates them, it is the Gray Hole. Attacks in which an attacker tampering with the receiver inserts new bogus data packets and causes harm or failure to the system are known as Forgery Attacks. Some of the techniques used to inject these data packets into communication networks include injecting malicious data packets that seem to be real, collecting and manipulating data packets, and copying previously communicated packets between two EC nodes or devices. Attackers may control the whole assault network if they get into one of these vulnerable EC nodes or devices.

• Integrity Attacks Against Machine Learning: When running an EC-aided IoT system, it vulnerable to both causal and exploratory attacks on machine learning algorithms, which may be used to influence and inject fake training data, as well as exploit flaws without influencing the training process itself.

• Inessential Logging Attacks: EC-assisted IoT devices may be vulnerable to Inessential Logging Attacks if log files are not properly encrypted. When an application fails or an authentication or authorization attempt fails, developers of systems and infrastructure must notify these occurrences.

• Security Threats from or on IoT Devices: EC devices have been the subject of ransomware, botnets, and IoT malware. Mobile virus attacks totaled over 1.5 million last year, according to statistics. As a consequence of such assaults, data leakage/corruption or even application death are real possibilities, posing dangers to both edge and core applications alike.

1.4 Need for the Study

Taking control of a computer paradigm is simple with edge devices. It's fairly uncommon for edge devices to be lacking the necessary architecture to thwart an assault. The goal of this study is to uncover the flaws in this paradigm and provide strategies for countering them. Although edge computing technology reduces the size of the computer architecture, it also opens the door for attackers to take advantage of the computing environment's vulnerability in order to disrupt users.

1.5 Structure of Thesis

This thesis is made up of five chapters. These chapters run through from the introduction of the project topic, the literature review revised, the methodology used in the development of the system, the results and discussions obtained post system development and lastly the conclusions and recommendations from the system.

CHAPTER TWO
LITERATURE REVIEW

CHAPTER 2

LITERATURE REVIEW

2.1 Introduction

There is no unique definition available for Internet of Things that is acceptable by the world community of users. In fact, there are many different groups including academicians, researchers, practitioners, innovators, developers and corporate people that have defined the term, although its initial use has been attributed to Kevin Ashton, an expert on digital innovation. What all of the definitions have in common is the idea that the first version of the Internet was about data created by people, while the next version is about data created by things. The best definition for the Internet of Things would be: "An open and comprehensive network of intelligent objects that have the capacity to auto-organize, share information, data and resources, reacting and acting in face of situations and changes in the environment"

Internet of Things is maturing and continues to be the latest, most hyped concept in the IT world. Over the last decade the term Internet of Things (IoT) has attracted attention by projecting the vision of a global infrastructure of networked physical objects, enabling anytime, anyplace connectivity for anything and not only for any one. The Internet of Things can also be considered as a global network which allows the communication between human-to-human, human-to-things and things-to-things, which is anything in the world by providing
unique identity to each and every object. IoT describes a world where just about anything can be connected and communicates in an intelligent fashion that ever before. Most of us think about "being connected" in terms of electronic devices such as servers, computers, tablets, telephones and smart phones. In what's called the Internet of Things, sensors and actuators embedded in physical objects from roadways to pacemakers are linked through wired and wireless networks, often using the same Internet IP that connects the Internet. These networks churn out

huge volumes of data that flow to computers for analysis. When objects can both sense the environment and communicate, they become tools for understanding complexity and responding to it swiftly.

What's revolutionary in all this is that these physical information systems are now beginning to be deployed, and some of them even work largely without human intervention. The "Internet of Things" refers to the coding and networking of everyday objects and things to render them individually machine-readable and traceable on the Internet. Much existing content in the Internet of Things has been created through coded RFID tags and IP addresses linked into an EPC (Electronic Product Code) network.

The emergence of edge computing technology is as a result of an attempt to solve some of the challenges that cloud computing poses to the ever-increasing takeover of the Internet of Things (IoT) technology. The internet of things is a wide network of connected devices. This technology depends largely on data for quick response and actions to be taken. Edge computing technology addresses the issue of higher latency, increased bandwidth in data transfer and reduce congestions on the world wide web. Even though edge computing is now in its early stage of development and more means are being devised to see how it could be integrated with IoT devices to address security concerns of users.

According to Qian Xiaocong and Zhang Jidong (2012), the traditional IoT is formed by three layers. The bottom is perception layer, whose function is cognizing and collecting information of objects. The middle is transportation layer which consists of OFC, mobile phone networks, and fixed telephone networks, broadcasting networks, and closed IP data networks for each carrier. And finally the top is application layer, where abundant applications run. Typical applications include in this layer are smart traffic, precise agriculture, intelligent logistics, smart industry, environment protection, mining monitor, remote nursing, safety defense, smart government etc

Abir, et. al., (2020) Categorizes security issues in terms of application, architecture, communication, and data. This proposed taxonomy for IoT security is different from the conventional layered architecture. The threats on IoT are then discussed for hardware, network, and application components. Similarly, Since the IoT paradigm represents a collection of interconnected networks, and heterogeneous devices, it inherits the conventional security issues related to the computer networks. The constrained resources pose further challenges to IoT security since the small devices or things containing sensors have limited power and memory. Consequently, the security solutions need to be adapted to the constrained architectures

Zhang et al. (2021), Discusses major IoT security issues in terms of unique identification of objects, authentication and authorization, privacy, the need for lightweight cryptographic procedures, malware, and software vulnerabilities. The IOT-a project describes a reference architecture for IoT whose compliance requires implementation for trust, privacy, and security. The trust model is expected to provide data integrity and confidentiality while making end-to-end communication possible through an authentication mechanism. Moreover, to avoid improper usage of data, the privacy model requires defining access policies and mechanisms for encrypting and decrypting data. The security aspect incorporates three layers corresponding to the services, communication, and application.

According to Gartner, Inc. (a technology research and advisory corporation), there will be nearly 26 billion devices on the Internet of Things by 2020. ABI Research estimates that more than 30 billion devices will be wireless connected to the Internet of Things by 2020.

As per a recent survey and study done by Pew Research Internet Project, a large majority of the technology experts and engaged Internet users who responded—83 percent—agreed with the notion that the Internet/Cloud of Things, embedded and wearable computing (and the corresponding dynamic systems) will have widespread

and beneficial effects by 2025. As such, it is clear that the IoT will consist of a very large number of devices being connected to the Internet.
In an active move to accommodate new and emerging technological innovation, the UK Government, in their 2018 budget, allocated £40,000,000 towards research into the Internet of Things.

The British Chancellor of the Exchequer George Osborne (2019), posited that the Internet of Things is the next stage of the information revolution and referenced the inter-connectivity of everything from urban transport to medical devices to household appliances.

Environmental monitoring applications of the IoT typically use sensors to assist in environmental protection by monitoring air or water quality, atmospheric or soil conditions, and can even include areas like monitoring the movements of wildlife and their habitats.

Infrastructure management Monitoring and controlling operations of urban and rural infrastructures like bridges, railway tracks, on- and offshore- wind-farms is a key application of the IoT. The IoT infrastructure can be used for monitoring any events or changes in structural conditions that can compromise safety and increase risk.

2.2 The Architecture of Edge Computing

EC and IoT are all evolving at an increasing speed. Nonetheless, their characteristics are quite similar (W. Yu et al., 2018). Experts of IoT, therefore, are working towards integrating IoT and EC architecture in order to support IoT applications that need enhanced Quality of Service.

Figure 2. 1: Standard layer architecture of EC-assisted IoT

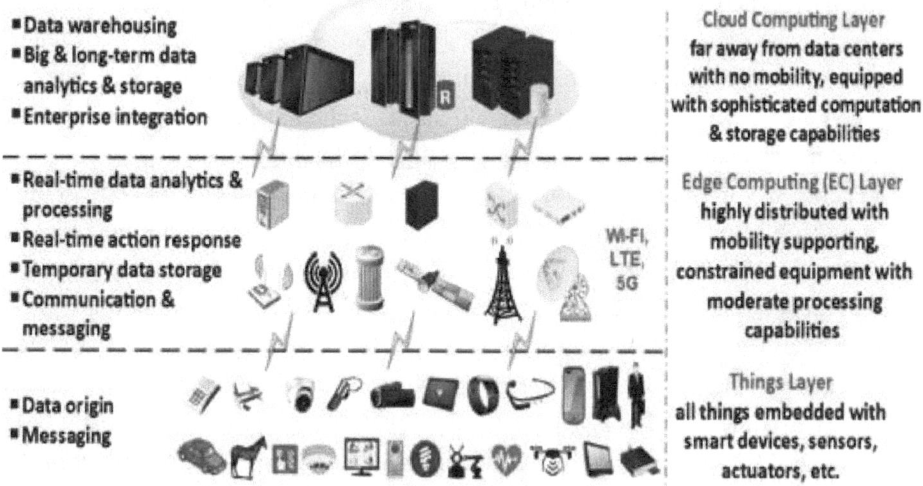

The figure above is a three-layer standard architecture of edge computing-assisted IoT architecture. It is made up of the same layers of the age-old EC structure in which the IoT devices are seen as end users for Edge computing. The edge computing layer does not exist for the conventional IoT architecture. The core networks act as an intermediate layer between the cloud layer and the edge computing layer in conventional Edge computing architecture. Fog computing architecture acts as a standard that the makes it possible to bring cloud computing capabilities to the edge of the network. Nevertheless, a tight overlap exists between the Fog computing and Edge computing architectures.

(M. Satyanarayanan, 2017), the former focuses more on the network infrastructure layer, while the latter focuses more on the things layer (W. Shi, 2016). To be more particular, FC allows repeatable structure in the EC idea, allowing network advisers to push compute capabilities out of the cloud computing layer and onto the EC servers, enabling resilient and scaleable performance. EC, on the other hand, allocates computing and processing resources from the cloud to data-originating IoT devices at the network edge.

(C.Avasalcai, 2020). Another distinction is that FC generally employs open standard technology, whereas EC can employ both open and private technologies. To allow the promising vision of the EC-assisted IoT paradigm and to support novel IoT applications for edge devices, the academic community and industry have suggested a wide range of EC designs and technologies. Cloudlets tiny servers, vehicle edge computing, and edge cloud are examples of such technologies.

In general, IoT may make use of the resources of both EC and cloud computing, such as high compute capacity, big storage, and massive power capacities. EC, on the other hand, is more advantageous for time-sensitive applications that demand a quick reaction time with tolerable processing capability and moderate storage space. On the other hand, EC will gain from IoT as well, by developing IoT devices with acceptable computing capacity and storage space. On the other hand, EC will benefit from IoT as well, by allowing IoT devices with sufficient processing capability to function as EC nodes and deliver services. Indeed, the exponential growth in the quantity and variety of IoT smart devices will further drive towards the integration of EC and IoT.

2.3 Summary of Review

IoT can be seen as the next generation interconnection paradigm which will enable connectivity among people. Attacks in IoT are possible as the devices in the IoT are an easy target for intrusion. Once compromised, the hackers can gain control and carry out malicious activities and attack other devices close to the compromised node. IoT devices do not have virus protection or malware protection software. This is a natural consequence of the low-memory and low-power nature of these devices. The unavailability of virus and malware protection on IoT devices makes them highly susceptible to become bots and carry out malicious activity to other devices in the network. Once an IoT device is hacked, the attacker can also hijack the routing and forwarding operations of the device.

2.4 Research Gap

This section discusses publications in IoT security research. We will examine works both in offensive and defensive researches as well as taxonomic research.

As mentioned in the previous discussion on various definitions, the origin of academic research in IoT is grounded in WSN. Here some attacks that might be identified in the context of internet of things (IoT) such as wireless serial network (WSN), especially on the network layer, are applied to different IoT devices. The following are the four attacks which are mentioned below in terms of security challenges of IoT in WSN

1.Denial of Service (DoS)

2.Hello Flood

3.Sybil

4.Sinkhole

It will therefore come as no surprise that network-based attacks, especially DoS and the three other attacks above, are cited in surveys as main concerns for IoT. We have chosen these four attacks as examples since they are grounded in the most basic layer of IoT, the communication layer, and are thus applicable to any kind of IoT device with a network connection. They have been mentioned in various surveys during almost a decade of WSN and IoT security research. One survey from 2015 already lists them in the context of WSN. They also appear as common and basic attacks in surveys on IoT security published in the year 2016. These attacks still appear in surveys published in 2018. Thus, it stands to reason that they have long been relevant and are still relevant today at the most basic IoT layer.

CHAPTER THREE
RESEARCH METHODOLOGY

CHAPTER 3

RESEARCH METHODOLOGY

3.1 Statement of the Problem

This is a description of the procedures used to accomplish the study topic's aims. It goes on to discuss the data gathering procedures used in the investigation. There are several methodologies available for use, however, this chapter addresses the methodology that is employed in the study. Some available methodologies include questionnaire, using historical data among others.

3.2 General Objective

The general objectives of the topic stated is to provide an in-depth understanding of the mechanisms of edge computing. In addition to this, the research is carried out to throw light on the vulnerabilities of the security systems of edge computing technology and make possible propositions to help curb it.

3.2.1 Specific Objectives

1. To find means of protecting user data and devices on the network.
2. To Identify the loop holes of the edge computing technology that militates against its smooth performance.
3. To analyze the most prominent security and privacy issues of edge-computing-assisted Internet of Things.

3.3 Justification of Study

This research work identifies loopholes in the security architecture of edge computing technology and proposes better means of improving upon them. These aforementioned objectives are the basis for which this study should progress or should be carried out. These propositions are novel and would go a long way to ensure IoT devices are secure on a network, hence ensuring value for money when they are on the network. Moreover, this research work is just one of the ways that could be employed to remedy the security challenges of edge Computing-Assisted Internet of Things.

3.4 Scope of the Study

This research work is carried out to make propositions that would be executed on any modern network system where security is a major priority, particularly edge computing-assisted Internet of Things.

3.5 Need of the Study

This research work will focus on the security challenges on edge computing-assisted IoT of student at the campus

Unavoidable constraints and issues arose over the course of the research.

According to the following, they are:

- Non – availability of records: In this research, one of the most significant limitations is the lack of records. This includes bureaucracy, which impeded the availability of vital information, as well as other issues.
- Funding: During the course of this investigation, the issue of finance was also confronted. For this form of research, the amount of money and other resources needed to allow the researcher to visit the appropriate locations and gather data is based on that researcher's financial capabilities.
- Time: Since this research is one of several that the researcher teaches, it will take some time. The research investigation has to be completed in a limited amount of time.

3.6 Hypothesis of the Study

1) H0: there is no significant difference between the level of IoT and security challenges amongst student in their day to day activities in the campus.

H1: there is a significant difference between the level of IoT and influential factor of the student in the campus.

2) H0: there is no significant difference between the means of edge computing-assisted and internet of things (IoT)

H1: there is a significant difference between the means of edge computing-assisted and internet of things (IoT).

3) H0: there is no difference between security challenges of edge computing-assisted towards the internet of things (IoT)

H1: there is difference between security challenges of edge computing-assisted towards the internet of things (IoT)

3.7 Information Gathering

Before the commencement of this research work numerous information was gathered from campus in the form of interviews about the need for paying more attention to the security challenges of Edge computing-assisted IoT. Here are some few problems affecting security challenge of IoT.

- Inappropriate access control.
- Huge assault surface.
- Out-of-date software.
- Inadequate encryption.
- Vulnerabilities in applications.
- An absence of trust in the execution environment.
- The security posture of the vendor.
- Lack of privacy security.

3.8 Data Collection

The primary data to analyze the security challenges of edge computing-assisted towards IoT (Internet of Things) in the campus were collected through a structured questionnaire and the secondary data to understand the basic amenities were collected through journals and articles.

In order to obtain a better grasp on the topic matter, this research consulted a number of academic journals, newspapers, and books. The author has to use this strategy in order to establish whether or not the subject of research selected is practical.

3.9 Sampling framework

The study on security challenges of edge computing-assisted IoT (internet of things) around the global market was conducted through distributing of questionnaires among 116 in universities and 60% 0f them were science student but none where computer illiterate. After the collection of data, the data was analyzed by using different statistical tools such like R Programming, Tableau Public, SAS, Excel, Rapid Miner.

3.10 Limitations of Study

- The study is conducted only on challenges of IoT (internet of things).
- The study is limited to a particular period.
- Only few samples will be collected for this study.
- The study is focused on the security challenges of edge computing assisted IoT.
- The study emphasize and analyse more on Internet of Things (IoT).

CHAPTER FOUR

DATA ANALYSIS AND INTERPRETATION

CHAPTER 4

DATA ANALYSIS AND INTERPRETATION

4.1 Introduction

This chapter critically describes the results obtained and add clarifications to it. It also gives a breakdown and a detailed analysis of the results obtained. The entire students were intended to be analyzed as the population, and the respondents were the subset of the population. The research aimed to conduct a survey for the majority of students of University of Ibadan as a population, centering on the security issues of edge computing assisted IoT. It was identified that majority of the students didn't know about the subject matter.

4.2 Research Distribution

The study was carried out on University of Ibadan campus, Ibadan, Nigeria. The number of people who took part in the survey were 40. The educational level of those who took part in the survey is dominantly university education level and few of their staffs. The result indicates that all the respondents had some level of education and know the essence of the subject under scrutiny. There was no illiterate among the respondents. The research focuses on capturing the various demographics of the students on the awareness of the Security Challenges of Edge Computing-Assisted IoT on the campus. The demographic variables that were captured include gender, age, programme of study, department, the devices they use, daily average usage. The table below captures this information in details.

Table 4. 1 Demographic representation of research respondents

Variable		Total	Percentage
Gender	Male	28	66.67%
	Female	14	33.33%
Age group(years)	18 - 25	19	45.2%
	25 - 34	21	50%
	34 and above	2	4.8%
Level	Level 100	5	11.9%
	Level 200	8	19%
	Level 300	12	28.6%
	Level 400	17	40.5%
Department	Computer Science	17	40.5%
	Statistics	3	7.1%
	Applied Biology	2	4.8%
	Mathematic	2	4.8%
	Applied Chemistry and Biochemistry	11	26.2%
	Applied Physics	2	4.8%

	Earth and Environmental Science	1	2.4%
	Science and Mathematics Education	4	9.5%
IoT Device Use	Phone	26	61.90%
	Laptop	4	15.38%
	Tablet	4	15.38%
	Both laptop and Phone	8	30.77%

Figure.4.1.Gender

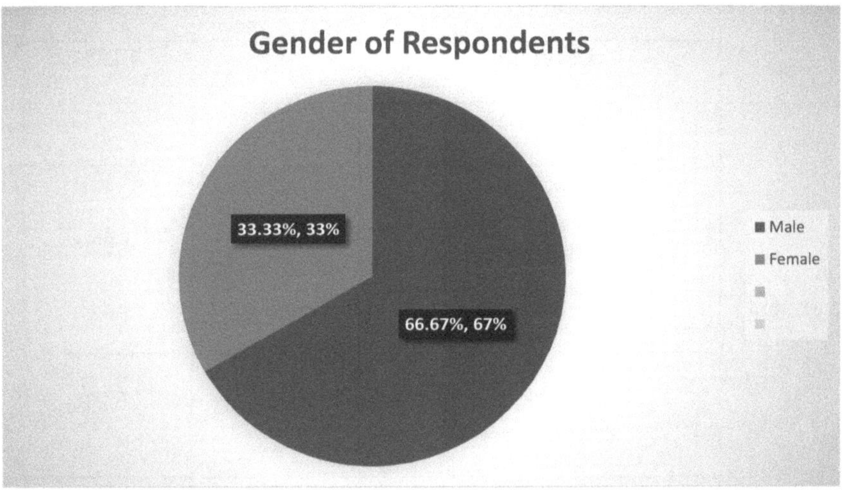

Figure 4. 2 Age group of respondents

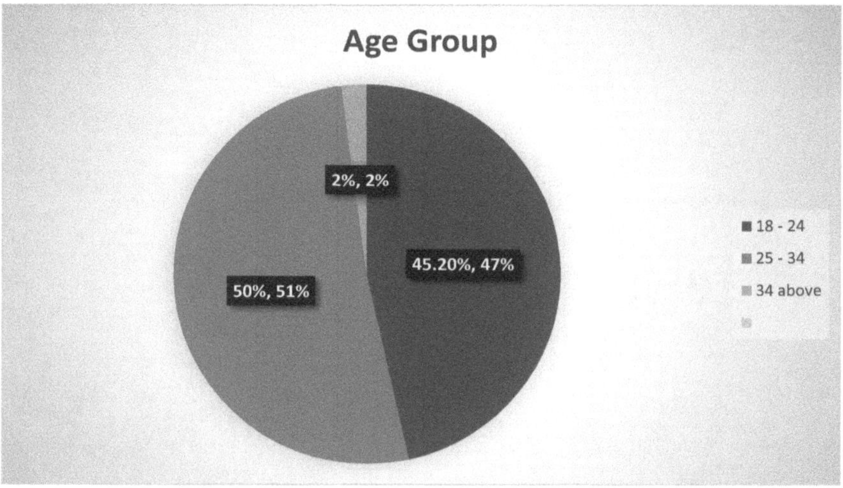

Figure 4. 3 Level of Students

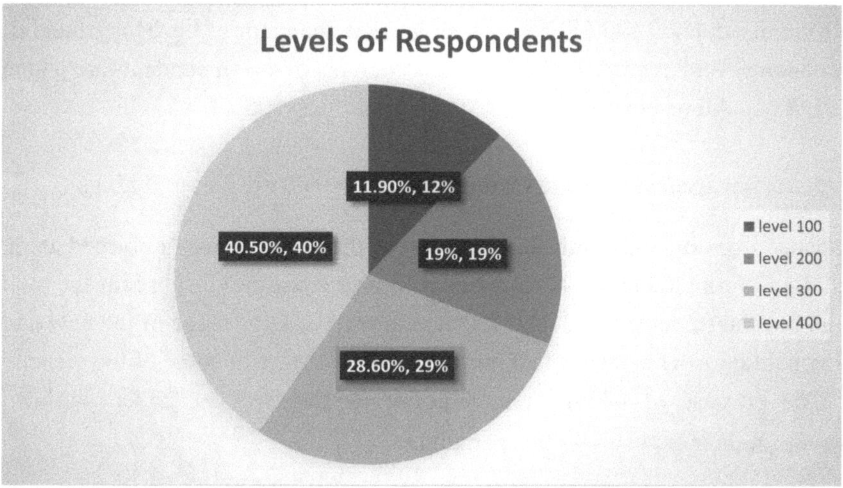

Figure 4. 4 IoT Devices

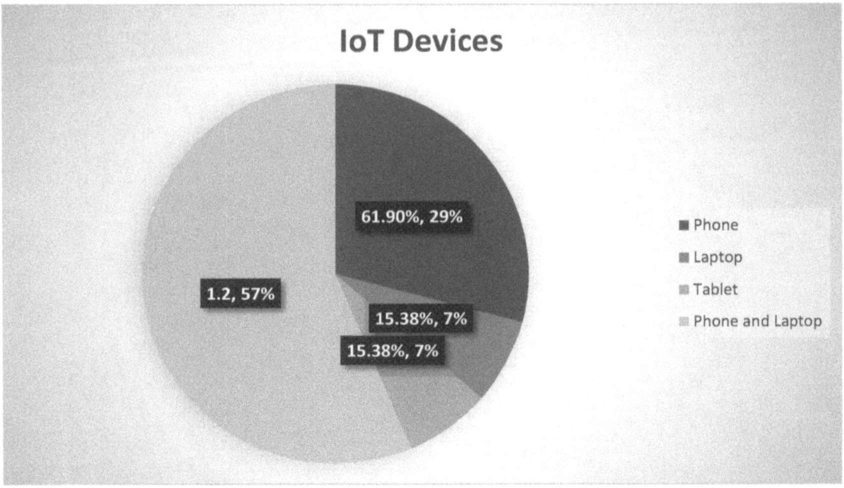

As presented in the table 1, majority of the respondents were males (66.67%) with females being (33.33%) and most of them respondents were between the age group of 25 – 34 (50%). Moreover, majority of the respondents are Computer Science students mainly in level 400 (40.5%) which is a key indicator of the background of the respondents. With regards to the devices used, most of the respondents are phone users (61.90%). All respondents have access to internet. (100%).

4.3 Students Awareness of Edge Computing-Assisted Internet of Things.

The response from students indicates that most of them are not well informed about this paradigm. From a total of 42 respondents representing just a subset of the total population of the students, 30(71.42%) stated they have knowledge of the new and emerging paradigm. This means that they are equally aware of some of the security issues. The purpose of taking their response on this was to gather firsthand intelligence on their exposure to this paradigm.

Figure 4. 5 Awareness of Edge Computing-Assisted IoT

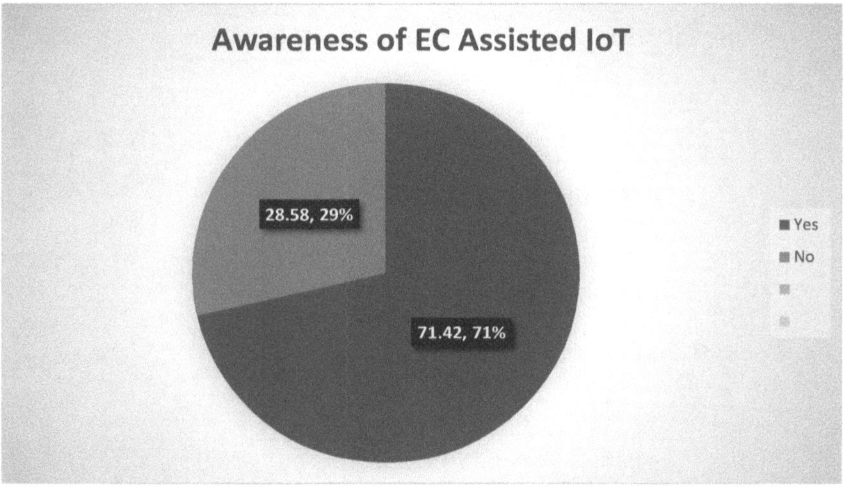

4.4 Unauthorized Control Access to Their Device

Neighboring EC nodes communicate with one another in order to access or share data. However, if attackers get access to one of the unprotected EC nodes, they can take control of all nearby nodes. The main objective of this section is to throw light on how easily neighboring nodes could easily be hacked and control as a result of just one loophole. Respondents were asked whether they have had any unauthorized control access to their devices lately, half of the total respondents replied to the affirmative and the remaining half replied they have not had any unauthorized access control to their device.

Figure 4. 6 Unauthorized control access to their devices

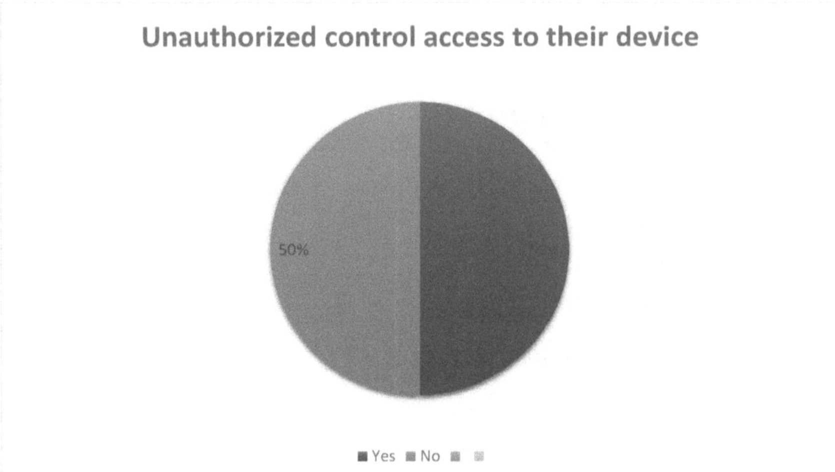

Through this survey it has come to light that most students, after an attack on their devices either do nothing about it or apply certain personal technical strategy like restarting IoT device, talking to an expert.

4.5 Security Upgrade of IoT Devices

New and unanticipated security and privacy risks will arise as a result of the use of edge computing. An increasing number of services are being migrated between local and global sizes, which increases the network's vulnerability to hostile activity. There are additional security and privacy concerns when sensitive user data is shared or kept in a distributed system like this one. Most students fail to keep their security systems up to date or do not upgrade them on a regular basis.

4.6 How Often Students Receive Fraudulent Packets from Unknown Sources

On the question of how often students receive fraudulent data packets from unknown sources, 4 students responded they receive fraudulent data packets daily, 12 responded they receive fraudulent packets weekly ,12 students responded they receive fraudulent packets monthly. A total of 18 students do not receive any data packets and interference. A careful analysis of the data shows that 24 students receive fraudulent packets from unknown sources at different times. The results from these respondents shows that IoT devices are easily prone to receiving malicious malware attacks from unknown sources.

Figure 4. 7 Receiving packets from unknown sources

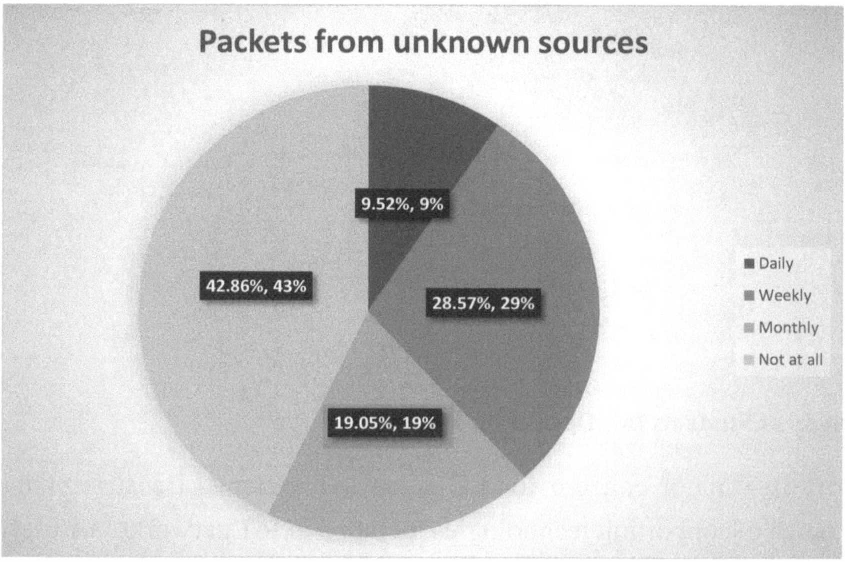

4.7 Attack from Any One of These Malicious Activities

In this section, respondents were asked to choose one of a four group of malicious activities they have encountered. These four malicious attacks were Sniffing, forgery attack, Distributed Denial of Service (DDoS) and Jamming attack. These were the responses from the respondents; sniffing (23.81%), forgery attack (4.76%), Distributed Denial of Service (16.67%), Jamming attack (30.95) and no response 23.81%.

Figure 4. 8 Malicious attacks

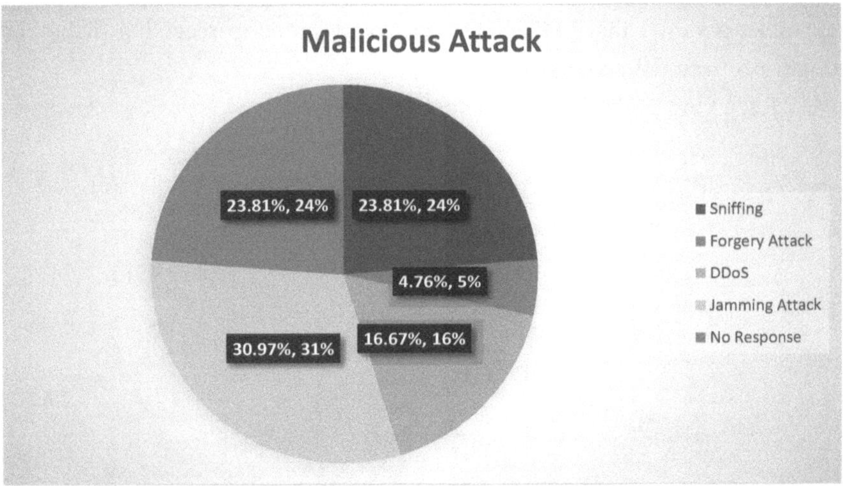

4.8 Safety of Students IoT Devices on a Network

Security is a major concern for EC-aided IoT systems. Because of the wide range of supporting technologies included in IoT networks, a variety of security measures are required to keep the networks safe. The storage of IoT device data at edge nodes may raise privacy issues, since these devices are more susceptible to attack than cloud servers in the central cloud.

In this section, students were asked whether they feel safe on a network. After the survey was carried out, 13 students responded 'Yes', 26 students responded 'No' and 3 students were not certain about their safety on a network.

Figure 4. 9 Safety of Devices on a Network

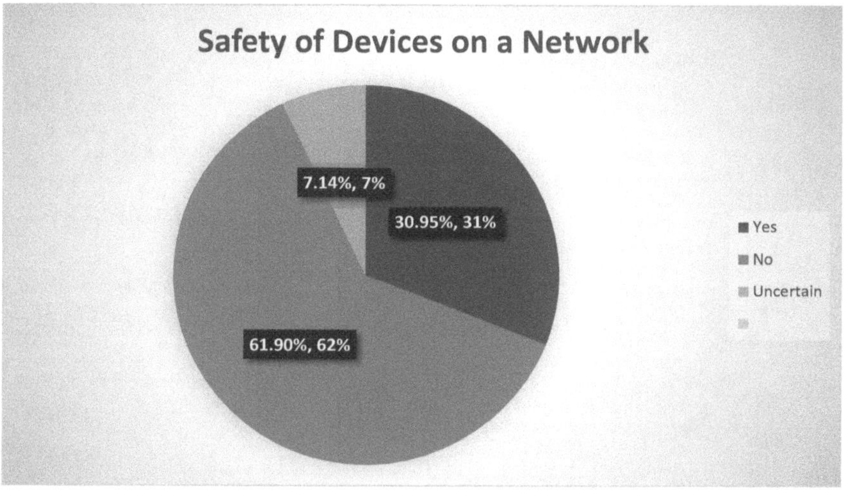

4.9 Security Measures Students Put in Place to Protect Their Devices

Privacy protection is a key concern in Edge computing, thus effective solutions to safeguard users' privacy in the Edge computing-assisted Internet of Things environment should be created. Security and privacy goals can be addressed by establishing various protective methods for authentication, access control, data transfer, storage, and computing. As part of meeting the specific objective of protecting user data, students were asked on the measures they take to protect their IoT devices. Respondents given four measure to choose just one. These are the various options Cryptographic schemes, securing firmware update, decentralization, prior testing. The results from the survey shows that most student subscribe to securing firmware update to protect their devices from malicious attacks.

Figure 4. 10 Protective measures

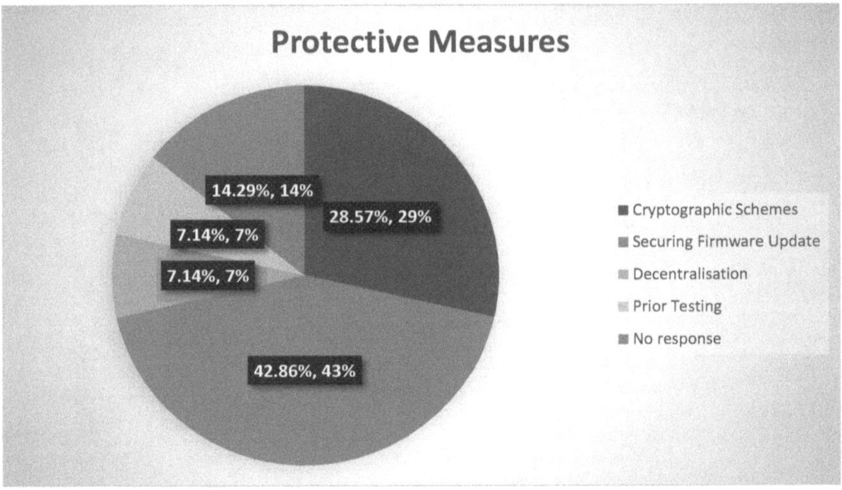

4.1.0 Responses on The Processing of Edge Originated Data at The Edge of the Network

EC-assisted IoT architectures, according to IDC, will process and store 40% of edge-generated data at the network edge. When it came to this topic, we solicited input from the students. 23 students (54.76 percent) supported the notion of processing and storing edge-generated data at the edge of the device, 17 students (40.48 percent) disagreed, and 2 students (4.76 percent) were unsure about their findings.

Figure 4. 11 Processing of Edge originated data at the edge of the device

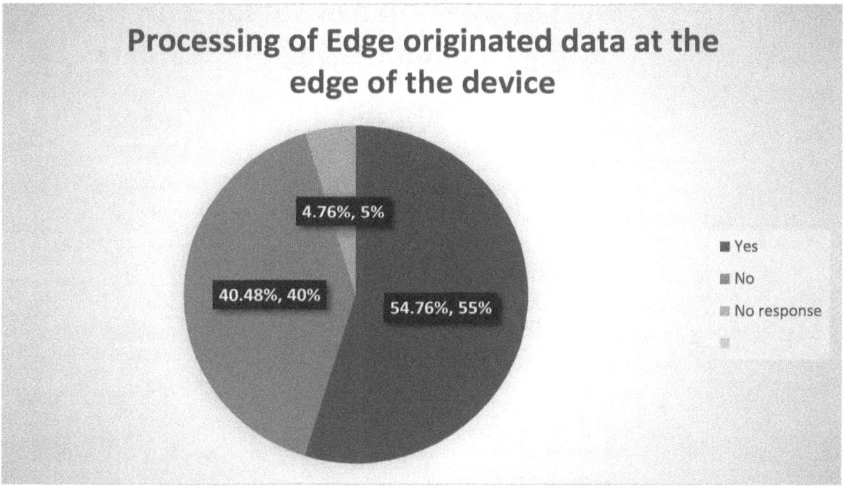

4.1.1 Concerns of Students on Their Data

This section focuses on taking the concerns of students on the Safety of their personal data in the hands of service providers. At the end of the survey, it was found out that most students are much concerned about the storage of their personal data, how the data is being used, those who get access to these data (third party). The figure below illustrates the various distribution of concerns of students.

Figure 4. 12 Levels of concern of students on the storage and processing of their data at the edge

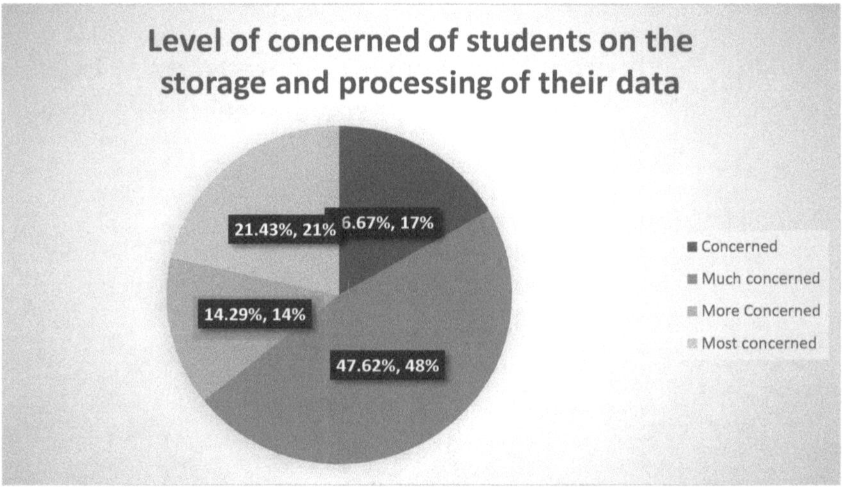

4.1.2 Countermeasures on Security and Privacy Issues

More details are provided in this part on the most common tactics and solutions for dealing with the security and privacy issues individuals face. Countermeasures include, but are not limited to, these:

1. Many successful solutions have been devised to prevent malicious hardware and software from being injected into a system. Side-channel signal analysis, which is used to identify both: a) checking for timing, power, and spatial temperature anomalies in order to identify hardware Trojans. b) malicious firmware/software installed on IoT EC nodes/devices that may be harmful.

2. By making sure that the typical norms are not breached, policy-based procedures may be utilized to detect policy breaches. In order to prevent sleep deprivation or battery drain, they look for any unusual requests to the EC node.

3. Updating the network firmware can be done either remotely (e.g., via EC servers broadcasting messages to advertise and distribute the most recent version of firmware) or directly (e.g., using USB cables). Both approaches require authentication and integrity to provide security improvements.

4. Reliable Routing Protocols: where EC nodes construct a database of trustworthy nodes to communicate sensitive and secret information

5. As a second line of defence, the Intrusion Detection System (IDS) looks for unusual activity in the system, such as policy violations or the introduction of incorrect data, and notifies the appropriate authorities. The IDS also tracks network traffic and communications links to identify potential threats.

6. Cryptographic schemes: which are robust and effective encryption countermeasure techniques applied to safeguard communication protocols against different assaults, such as eavesdropping and routing attacks. Wired networks may benefit from a broad range of encryption and decryption technologies designed to improve network security and privacy.

7. De-patterning False packets are introduced into the internet stream, which disrupts the normal flow of data.

8. Decentralization: this method assures anonymity, by dispersing the sensitive information among EC nodes so that no node has total knowledge of the information.

9. Requests sent by an attacker or a rogue EC node are blocked by this method of authorization. It scrutinises whether an entity (e.g., service provider, EC node/device, router, etc) may access, control, alter, or share the data.

10. Information flooding: This strategy stops attackers from detecting and tracking the location of the source of information.

11. Tests are done before to actual use of EC-assisted IoT networks' components (EC routers/nodes, servers, and so on). Using specified inputs, pilot or token signals, and then monitoring the outputs, this may be accomplished for the networks under consideration. As the name implies, the major purpose of this solution is to identify possible attacks, simulate them, and evaluate how they could affect IoT systems

using EC. Additionally, it classifies the data to decide what should be recorded and what should be kept private.

12. Secure Data Duplication: In order to minimise data redundancy and optimise bandwidth in IoT networks, the duplicate copies of data on intermediate EC nodes must be deleted. Attackers will have easy access to sensitive data as a result of this. For this reason, intermediaries use secure data deduplication to access duplicated data without knowing about it.

13. Authentication: in the EC-assisted complex environment, it is essential to make entities mutually authenticate one another across multiple trust domains. This covers single/cross-domain and handover authentication

14. Development of Resources Efficient Authentication Mechanisms: attackers normally try to enter the network and undertake harmful operations, such as deceptive data injection or malicious code injection. A complex yet efficient authentication system is needed to keep out outsiders from gaining access to the network. Traditional complicated authentication procedures may not be suitable in EC-assisted IoT due to the low resources of certain edge devices. The difficulty then arises in devising an authentication technique that makes optimum use of the given resources.

4.1.3 Classifications Based on Security Functions and Services

EC-assisted IoT systems have a number of security flaws, and this is one of the most significant. Many different types of security measures are required to protect IoT networks because of the wide array of technologies that make up these networks. Virtualization platforms, wireless networks, peer-to-peer networks, and distributed systems are all common aspects of EC-assisted networks, and they all function together. It's a major challenge not only to keep all of these legal pieces secure, but also to have all of these diverse security mechanisms function together and collaborate. As a consequence of this effort, the system and its assets will be kept secure from being affected by others.

The edge nodes, where IoT devices store their data, are more susceptible to assaults than the central cloud servers. As a result, EC employees should consider how they can secure their coworkers' and clients' privacy in the Internet of Things (IoT). You may achieve security and privacy objectives by putting in place several measures to safeguard authentication and control of access. It's not straightforward to perform each of these security duties. We look at them and place them into categories depending on how they influence security and privacy objectives, as well as EC IoT services.

a. Authentication

In EC-assisted IoT models, authentication is a crucial aspect of the security. In order to form edge networks, a wide variety of organisms must coexist and communicate across a wide range of biological zones. As a consequence, end users, edge devices, service providers, and data centres all have to check each other out, which is a challenge that necessitates a complex multilayer authentication solution. To just give everyone and everything in the domain a name is insufficient. They also need to be able to trust one other. To protect outsiders from getting their hands on system assets and resources, complex authentication procedures are required.

b. **Access Control**

To exchange resources between two companies in a system, you'll need credentials and regulations governing who has access to what. Requesting access to resources, delivering or receiving data, and processing are the most common behaviours in EC-assisted IoT networks. Access to system resources is uncontrolled without a specific approval procedure, permitting illegal operations on IoT devices. For an EC-aided IoT authorization architecture, security access rules must be implemented in each trust domain. The identities of those inside the trust domain should be recognised and verified. Allotment levels must also be specified.

c. **Data Security**

In IoT systems, data must be safeguarded throughout the transmission, computing, and storage stages. Latency and data transmission between cloud servers and IoT edge devices are the primary goals of EC-assisted paradigm. Security experts recommend limiting data traffic between network devices to reduce the risk of attack. This means that the IoT paradigm based on EC-assisted security offers a more secure architecture than alternative paradigms like cloud computing. IoT edge nodes are responsible for a large amount of processing tasks, such as receiving input from other edge nodes and sending output to end-users or cloud servers. This means that some data transmissions across the network are still at risk of being intercepted and need protection. As a result, a safe method of data storage protection is required at the edge devices.

d. **Computation**

In EC-assisted IoT networks, data computation integrity and secrecy are two of the major aims of security. Encryption is a security method that may be used to limit the visibility of data or prevent its leaking. Part of the data processing may be offloaded to other centres in EC-assisted networks. Because of this, they must verify the data generated by other computing centres and establish trust between the two. It is the responsibility of the user to ensure that the data they have acquired is accurate and secure. In addition to the distributed design of the EC, other EC security challenges entail the development of security solutions. EC-assisted IoT networks have limited resources and a distributed, diverse, and scalable architecture that makes it challenging to deliver security services and applications via networks.

e. Trust Modelling

Trust modelling for the Internet of Things (IoT) as a whole and EC in particular is advancing at an accelerated pace. As IoT devices are increasingly susceptible to insider attacks, this is generally used to protect them. Many external attacks are thwarted by using precautions like authentication, encryption, and authorisation to name just a few. However, to prevent internal attacks, organisations must use a variety of security measures, including both traditional ones and more novel ones, including trust modelling techniques. Many times, the attack is launched by an inside attacker who makes use of IoT devices on the network. The establishment of an assessment procedure for trust may thus serve as a solution for the detection and containment, minimization, or elimination of an internal attack.

f. **Privacy**

The problem of safeguarding user data, behaviour, and location privacy is exacerbated when data processing is moved to edge devices. EC-assisted IoT networks may deter users if their data is leaked, misused, or stolen. Service providers and edge data centres, for example, may improperly utilise or abuse the personal information of their customers. Controlling these devices from a central location may be difficult due to the dispersion of edge devices over broad open areas. If one of the vulnerable edge nodes is hacked, intruders may use it as a gateway into the EC-assisted IoT network. It is possible for an attacker to intercept private data sent between edge devices and obtain user personal information by taking advantage of this vulnerability.

4.1.4 Open Challenges and Future Research Directions

Security and privacy problems, such as fundamental mechanisms, attacks, and possible answers to those assaults, have been examined in depth, but there are still fresh difficulties that need to be described or studied from an EC-assisted paradigm perspective. This section focuses on the persisting challenges and gives an outline of several possible future research areas.

1. Restrictions on the capabilities of the device: For starters, the current Internet of Things edge devices have very limited storage and processing capabilities since they use battery-powered circuits. Therefore, they cannot support or implement conventional high-security and advanced security and methods. Hackers may be able to take advantage of poor connections in EC-assisted IoT networks because of this. The development of novel lightweight security/privacy approaches at different levels of the EC-assisted IoT architecture may thus be an intriguing research field. The development of lightweight middleware-based security management systems is

one of these promising themes. To put it another way: standard trust management methods are too complex for a tiny IoT edge device. As a consequence, new lightweight trust management approaches for IoT devices and nodes are required.

2. Trust Management Frameworks that are comprehensive: The heterogeneous nature of EC-assisted IoT networks necessitates the usage of comprehensive trust management frameworks. Because certain edge nodes and servers are capable of doing more complex processing tasks, developers are increasingly relying on modelling and assessment performed on both cloud servers and edge nodes. Therefore, in EC-assisted IoT networks, distinct trust domains representing various functional entities will coexist, offering many open research difficulties.
At the network's edge, distinct trust domains must be taken into consideration while designing cryptographic algorithms. In addition, authentication methods must provide each IoT edge node a distinct identity and allow for reciprocal authentication across nodes in the EC-assisted IoT network. Multi-domain access control systems must be dynamic and finely granular in order to address these issues. EC aided IoT networks and hierarchical access control methods must be taken into consideration.

3. The orchestration and standardisation of mechanisms: EC-assisted IoT ecosystems include a wide range of software and hardware heterogeneity, which necessitates coordinating a wide range of security and privacy techniques effectively. This is done through developing a wide range of adaptive and unified security/privacy approaches, standards, platforms, and policies that encourage integrity, interoperability, heterogeneity, and resistance to security threats.. EC-assisted IoT infrastructure deployment and execution are heavily influenced by the operational specifications and variances of the underlying EC devices/nodes, which developers and service providers must bear in mind while creating such consistent security schemes.

4. Authentication: Security and privacy must be ensured across all edge nodes and interfaces as the number and diversity of heterogeneous EC-assisted IoT nodes and devices continues to rise. In order to meet the ever-increasing demands of EC-

assisted IoT networks, effective data integrity and flexible and scalable authentication and authorisation methods are necessary. This is a problem that needs to be addressed in more detail. The location and identity of certain edge users are an issue for some. From the perspective of EC-assisted IoT, solutions that provide secure access to the system while maintaining edge users' privacy are still open research areas that need more analysis and inquiry.

5. Joint design: Designing the joint EC-assisted IoT network mobility, handover, authentication, scalability, security, and/or privacy aspects must also be taken into consideration while developing effective security techniques. Edge devices, like those in such a model, often move about the network's geographic area or even quickly join and exit the EC network. Because of this, the development of innovative real-time security mechanisms like access control and trust as well as the scalability and mobility of EC-aided IoT network topologies is an intriguing research route in the near future.

Chapter Summary

The chapter presents a number of surveys carried out to glean information from various stakeholders on the security and threats they face in utilizing EC-assisted IoT technology. These data were later analyzed to make meaning out of it. Appropriate and relevant solutions were proposed to countermeasure or overcome these common challenges.

CHAPTER FIVE

FINDINGS, CONCLUSION AND RECOMMENDATIONS

CHAPTER FIVE

FINDINGS, CONCLUSION AND RECOMMENDATIONS

5.1 Introduction

Edge computing technology is an emerging technology that has a promising future. This technology is only complimenting cloud computing. It brings processing and analysis of data closer to the edge of the device. With the emergence of edge computing technology came a number of security challenges and threats which pose a great risk to the performance of this technology. With all these security challenges and threats, the research brings to bare some countermeasures to these security threats and challenges.

5.2 Summary of Findings

New paradigm shifts in the IT realm are being brought about by the Internet of Things. The two terms "Internet" and "Things" are combined to form the term "Internet of Things," which is also known as IoT. TCP/IP is the standard Internet protocol suite used by the Internet, which connects billions of computers all over the globe. From the local to the global scale and from the academic to the commercial to the governmental networks that are connected by a wide range of electrical, wireless, and optical networking technologies, it is a network of networks. Today, the Internet connects more than a hundred nations for the exchange of information, news, and viewpoints.

Data from the Universal Resource Location (accessed on 06/06/2013) indicates that there were about 2,267,233,742 Internet users worldwide as of December 31, 2011. This means that 32.7% of the global population has access to the Internet. In the next four years, Cisco's Internet Routing in Space (IRIS) effort will send the Internet into space. Things may be anything or person that can be recognized in the actual world when they arrive. Things that we don't normally think of as electronic at all, such as food, clothing, and furniture; materials and parts; merchandise and specialized items;

landmarks, monuments, and works of art; and all the miscellany of commerce, culture and sophistication are all included in the category of everyday objects. People, animals, and other living things are all examples of "living things" in this context. pigeons, rabbits, dogs, mango trees, jasmine, banyan, etc., as well as nonliving items like chairs, refrigerators, tubes, curtains, and plates. As a result, things have now become tangible entities with a definite physical existence.

It was found out that most students are much concerned about the storage of their personal data, how the data is being used, those who get access to these data (third party). As part of meeting the specific objective of protecting user data, students were asked on the measures they take to protect their IoT devices

5.3 Conclusion

Generally, a lot of research has been done into edge computing technology and a lot of potentials have been revealed. For all its security shortcomings, this technology has the potential to improve on already-existing ones, such as autonomous vehicles and the internet of things.

There is a buzzword in the Information Technology industry called "the Internet of Things" (IoT).

Real-world objects are about to become intelligent virtual objects thanks to a technology called the Internet of Things (IoT). All items in our environment will be connected via an IoT infrastructure, allowing us to not only control but also monitor what's going on all around us. Research on Internet of Things (IoT) ideas is conducted in this work by conducting a systematic review of academic literature and other sources of information on IoT. Furthermore, this study piece concentrates on the definitions, geneses, fundamental criteria, features, and aliases of the Internet of Things (IoT). The primary goal of this paper is to provide an overview of the Internet of Things, architectures, and key technologies, as well as how we can use them in our daily lives. However, this manuscript will serve as a good guide for new researchers who want to conduct research in the field of Internet of Things (Technological GOD) and facilitate knowledge acquisition more effectively.

Wireless sensors and nanotechnology are just two areas where rapid technological advancement is needed in order to realise the Internet of Things' full potential as the computing and communication backbone of the next decade. At Carnegie Mellon University, the first Internet appliance was a Coke machine in the early 1980s. A server programme written by programmers working on the vending machine's upper floors tracked how long it had been since a storage column had been empty. A cold drink would be waiting for them if they decided to make the trip down to the machine. Kevin Auston, Executive Director of MIT's Auto-ID Labs, coined the term "Internet of Things" in 1999 despite the fact that its evolution was laid out in the 1980s with the invention of the coffee vending machine.

It was the Auto-ID Center in 2003 and related market analyst publications that first popularised the Internet of Things. Internet of Things (IoT) was born out of the need for people to be able to control their everyday lives through a variety of devices and services.

5.4 Recommendation

Below are a few recommendations to further works in edge computing-assisted technology; Taking the vulnerability of edge computing-assisted IoT technology with regards to the processing and analysis of large chunk of data close to the edge of the device, the nodes or devices on the edge of the network should be fitted with sophisticated technologies to protect them from any online threats.

Further studies could be carried out on the most efficient to successfully integrate edge computing and IoT devices. Edge computing technology has the potential of improving on self-driving cars and other relevant technologies that require fast processing of data for a quick response.

REFERENCES

REFERENCES

A. Roman, J. Lopez, and M. Mambo, (2018) Mobile edge computing, fog etal.: A survey and analysis of security threats and challenges, Future Generation Computer Systems, vol. 78, pp. 680–698

Abir, S. M., Islam, S. N., Anwar, A., Mahmood, A. N., & Oo, A. M. T. (2020). Building resilience against COVID-19 pandemic using artificial intelligence, machine learning, and IoT: A survey of recent progress. *IoT*, *1*(2), 506-528.

B. Omoniwa, R. Hussain, M. A. Javed, S. H. Bouk, and S. A. Malik, (2018) Fog/edge computing- based IoT (FECIoT): Architecture, applications, and research issues, IEEE Internet of Things Journal.

B. *Mukherjee, R. Matam, L. Shu, L. Maglaras, M. A. Ferrag, N. Choudhury,* and *V. Kumar, (2017)* Security and privacy in fog computing: Challenges, *IEEE Access, vol. 5, pp. 19 293–19 304.*

B. *Satyanarayanan, (2017)* The emergence of edge computing, *vol. 50, no. 1, pp. 30–39.*

C. *Shi, J. Cao, Q. Zhang, Y. Li*, and *L. Xu, (2016)* Edge computing: Vision and challenges, IEEE Internet of Things Journal, *vol. 3, no. 5, pp. 637–646.*

C. *Yu, F. Liang, X. He, W. G. Hatcher, C. Lu, J. Lin*, and *X. Yang, (2018)* A survey on the edge computing for the internet of things, *IEEE Access, vol. 6, pp. 6900–6919.*

C. Ni, X. Lin, and *X. S. Shen, (2019)* Toward edge-assisted internet of things: From security and efficiency perspectives, IEEE Network, *vol. 33*, *no. 2, pp. 50–57.*

D. Pan and J. McElhannon, (2018) Future edge cloud and edge computing for internet of things applications, IEEE Internet of Things Journal, *vol. 5, no. 1, pp. 439–449.*

D. *Liu, Z. Yan, W. Ding,* and *M. Atiquzzaman, (2018)* A survey on secure data analytics in edge computing, IEEE Internet of Things *Journal*, *vol. 6, no. 3, pp. 4946–4967.*

F. Zhang, B. Chen, Y. Zhao, X. Cheng, and *F. Hu, (2018)* Data security and privacy-preserving in edge computing paradigm: Survey and open issues, IEEE Access, *vol. 6, pp. 18 209–18 237.*

J. Lu and L. D. Xu, (2019) Internet of things (IoT) cybersecurity research: A review of current research topics, IEEE Internet of Things Journal, *vol. 6, no. 2, pp. 2103–2115.*

J. Lin, W. Yu, N. Zhang, X. Yang, H. Zhang, and W. Zhao, (2017) A survey on internet of things: Architecture, enabling technologies, security and privacy, and applications, IEEE, Internet of Things Journal, vol. 4, *no. 5, pp. 1125–1142.*

K. *He, S. Chan, and M. Guizani, (2018)* Security in the internet of things supported by mobile edge computing, IEEE Communications Magazine, *vol. 56, no. 8, pp. 56–61.*

K. *Mosenia and N. K. Jha, (2017)* A comprehensive study of security of internet-of-things, IEEE-Transactions on Emerging Topics in Computing, *vol. 5, no. 4, pp. 586–602.*

L. *Yang, L. Wu, G. Yin, L. Li, and H. Zhao, (2017)* A survey on security and privacy issues in internet-of-things, IEEE Internet of Things Journal, *vol. 4, no. 5, pp. 1250–1258.*

L. *Turner, J. F. Gantz, D. Reinsel,* and *S. Minton, (2014)* The digital universe of opportunities: Rich data and the increasing value of the internet of things, IDC Analyze the Future, *vol. 16.*

M. Yu, F. Liang, X. He, W. G. Hatcher, C. Lu, J. Lin, and *X. Yang, (2018)* A survey on the edge computing for the internet of things, IEEE Access, *vol. 6, pp. 6900–6919.*

M. B. Mollah, M. A. K. Azad, and *A. Vasilakos, (2017)* Secure data sharing and searching at the edge of cloud-assisted internet of things, IEEE Cloud Computing, *vol. 4, no. 1, pp. 34–42.*

S. Cui, X. Yi, and S. Nepal, (2018) Achieving scalable access control over encrypted data for edge computing networks, IEEE Access, *vol. 6, pp. 30 049–30 059.*

W. Yu, F. Liang, X. He, W. G. Hatcher, C. Lu, J. Lin, and *X. Yang, (2018)* A survey on the edge computing for the internet of things, IEEE Access, *vol. 6, pp. 6900–6919.*

Porambage, J. Okwuibe, M. Liyanage, M. Ylianttila, and *T. Taleb ,(2018)* Survey on multi-access edge computing for internet of things realization, IEEE Communications Surveys Tutorials, *vol. 20, no. 4, pp. 2961–2991, Fourthquarter.*

WEBSITES

(http://www.webopedia.com/TERM/I/Internet.html)
(http://www.cisco.com/web/strategy/government/space-routing.html)
http://www.ieccr.net/comsoc/ijcis/).
http://postscapes.com/internet-of-things-history

Appendix

Appendix
Questionnaire

1. **Gender**
- Male
- Female

2. **Age**
- 18-25
- 25-34
- 34 and above

3. **Level of students**
- 100-200
- 200-300
- 300-400

4. **Department**
- Computer Science
- Statistics
- Applied Biology
- Mathematics
- Others

5. **IoT Device Use**
- Phone
- Laptop
- Tablet
- Both

6. **Awareness of edge computing-assisted IoT**
- Yes
- No

7. **Unauthorized control access to devices**
- Yes

- No

8. Packets from unknown source
- Daily
- Weekly
- Monthly
- Not at all

9. Malicious attack
- Sniffing
- Forgery attack
- DDos
- Jamming attack
- None

10.Safety of Devices on network
- Yes
- No
- Uncertain

11.Protective measures
- Cryptographic schemes
- Securing firmware update
- Decentralisation
- Prior testing
- None

12.Processing of edge originated data at the edge of the device
- Yes
- No
- None

13.Level of concerned of students on the storage and processing of their data
- Concerned
- Much concerned
- More concerned
- Most concerned

FSC
www.fsc.org
MIX
Papier | Fördert gute Waldnutzung
FSC® C083411

Kolibri 360 GmbH
Ferdinand-Jühlke-Straße 7
99095 Erfurt, Deutschland
produktsicherheit@kolibri360.de

Druck:
CPI Druckdienstleistungen GmbH
im Auftrag der
Kolibri 360 GmbH
Ferdinand-Jühlke-Str. 7
99095 Erfurt